THE

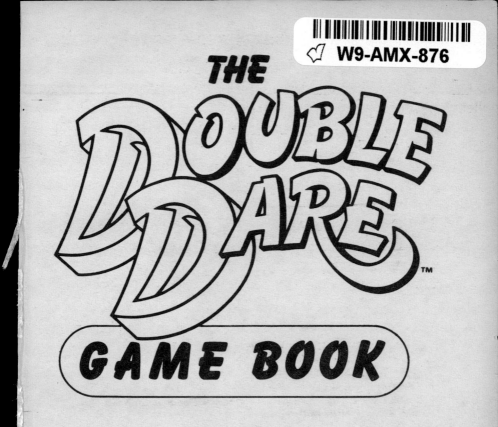

DOUBLE DARE ™

GAME BOOK

by Daniella Burr

PARACHUTE
PRESS, INC.

ISBN: 0-938753-40-1

PARACHUTE PRESS, INC.
200 FIFTH AVENUE
NEW YORK, NY 10010

First printing: October 1988
Printed in the USA

Design by Michel Design

CONTENTS

Marc Summers and a DOUBLE DARE team in a mess of fun.

CAN YOU ANSWER
THESE QUESTIONS?

Is *cometophobia* the fear of comets—or the fear of scrubbing sinks?

In Greek mythology is a *Hydra* a many-headed monster or a cream-filled cookie?

ARE YOU READY...

to tackle physical challenges with names like "I Want My Mummy," "Attack of the Killer Marshmallows," and "Back to Drool"?

Of course you are. You're a DOUBLE DARE™ fan, and you're set to dive into *THE DOUBLE DARE GAME BOOK* like an obstacle-course contestant dives into a tank of gak!

THE DOUBLE DARE GAME BOOK is the Official Handbook for all DOUBLE DARE fans. Just like your favorite TV game show, *THE DOUBLE DARE GAME BOOK* is loaded with official DOUBLE DARE questions. *And* just like on DOUBLE DARE, when the going gets tough—the tough get *super sloppy!* Check out the physical challenges in Chapters Two and Three, and you'll see what *that* means.

1

And if you survive those, there are top-secret, behind-the-scenes DOUBLE DARE Fast Facts, and a chewy chapter of daringly delicious DOUBLE DARE recipes. So much to do, you may feel like celebrating! No wonder there's a whole chapter on how to throw your own official DOUBLE DARE party!

You'll find page after page of DOUBLE DARE action no matter how you use this book. The first part of the book is set up like a real DOUBLE DARE game. Play the game on your own. See how many points you can rack up. Or play against a pal. The player with the most points at the end of a round is the winner. Or, you can get a group together and divide into teams—just like on TV!

Best of all, you can just flip through the book any time you feel like it. Quiz yourself with some of the questions. Test your skill with a few super sloppy stunts. Make a super snack from the double-delicious recipes. It's all up to you!

Ready to begin?

On your mark, get set, go!

We DOUBLE DARE you!

Chapter One

THE QUESTIONS

To answer or not to answer — that is the question about the questions on DOUBLE DARE. This chapter is filled with actual DOUBLE DARE questions that were asked on the show! Each page has four of them. The first two are DARE questions. Try one of them first. They are worth 20 points. If you can't answer the DARE questions, you can try a DOUBLE DARE question for double the points. (The answers are upside down at the bottom of the page.)

Or if the questions aren't your style, you can try the physical challenge. Just follow the instructions on the bottom of the page. They'll lead you to the physical challenges and a mess of fun! Since most of the physical challenges have time limits, you'll need a watch or clock with a second hand. And a pad and pencil will make it easy to keep score.

When you finish a physical challenge, check the instructions at the bottom of that page. They'll tell you what page to go to next and how to keep track of your score. That's all there is to it.

To answer or not to answer . . . that is the
question on **DOUBLE DARE.**

Hurry, hurry, hurry! Step right up! There's a question on this page that is just right for you. But choose one quick, they're going fast.

DARE

1. What famous book is about a pig named Wilbur and a spider named Charlotte?

2. What material comes from the cocoon of the silkworm?

DOUBLE DARE

1. When he was a teenager, what high school did Clark Kent (alias Superman) attend?
- A. Smallville High
- B. Horrible High
- C. Erasmus Hall High

2. What famous book is about four sisters named Meg, Jo, Beth, and Amy?

If you don't want to risk answering one of these questions, you can try the physical challenge instead. There's a good one waiting for you on page 26!

There's a good one waiting for you on page 26!

Give yourself 40 points for the right answer.
2. *Little Women*
DOUBLE DARE: 1. A. Smallville High
Give yourself 20 points for the right answer.
2. Silk
DARE: 1. *Charlotte's Web*
Answers:

You're such a DOUBLE DARE super star, you're sure to shine when you answer these questions!

DARE

1. When the band plays "Hail to the Chief," everyone stands and looks at the door. That's because someone special is coming. "Hail to the Chief" is the official song for what world leader?

2. What cartoon rodent starred in *Steamboat Willie* in 1928?

DOUBLE DARE

1. Calling all workout champs. If you are trying to build your triceps, are you working on your arms or legs?

2. What is the only letter not found in the names of any of the 50 United States?

Don't want to answer the question? Well, a star like you can do what you like—as long as you like physical challenges. There's one just for you on page 27.

Give yourself 40 points for the right answer.
2. Q
DOUBLE DARE: 1. Arms
Give yourself 20 points for the right answer.
2. Mickey Mouse
DARE: 1. The President of the United States
Answers:

Put on your thinking caps (you get to wear a lot of hats on DOUBLE DARE). Any question you choose is sure to be a stumper!

DARE
1. Are Clumsy, Brainy, and Harmony three of Snow White's dwarfs?

2. Into how many chambers is your heart divided?

DOUBLE DARE
1. True or false: The Empire State Building is the tallest building in the world.

2. It's once upon a time, time. According to Hans Christian Andersen's "The Little Mermaid," what do mermaids become when they die?
    A. Foam on the sea
    B. Stars in the sky
    C. Guests on DOUBLE DARE

If you've been stumped, there's a physical challenge on page 28 that's waiting for you.

~~~~~~~~~~~~~~~~~~~~~~~~~~~~~~~~~~~~~

Answers:
DARE: 1. No, they are Smurfs.
2. Four
Give yourself 20 points for the right answer.
DOUBLE DARE: 1. False.
2. A. Foam on the sea
Give yourself 40 points for the right answer.

7

DOUBLE DARE is the game show that offers you a choice! You have the chance to choose from any of these questions.

DARE

1. What did Yankee Doodle call the feather in his cap?

2. What two words are combined to form the word *brunch*?

DOUBLE DARE

1. *Aspartame* is the scientific name for what?
   A. Asparagus
   B. Aspergum
   C. NutraSweet

2. True or false: Drums and pianos are both percussion instruments.

If these questions are so tough they leave you speechless, try the physical challenge on page 30.

try the physical challenge on page 30.

Answers:
DARE: 1. Macaroni
2. *Breakfast and lunch*
Give yourself 20 points for the right answer.
DOUBLE DARE: 1. C. NutraSweet
2. True
Give yourself 40 points for the right answer.

Come on, be a sport! Try one of these questions!

DARE
1. In what sport could the Phillies play the Mets?

2. What is basketball-great Dr. J's first name?
A. Julius
B. Joanne
C. Johnny

DOUBLE DARE
1. What is the name of the very first play in any football game?

2. On the old *Bill Cosby Show,* what famous TV personality played gym teacher Chet Kincaid?

If you're in a sporting mood, check out the physical challenge on page 31.

~~~~~~

Answers:
DARE: 1. Baseball
2. A. Julius (his last name is Erving)
Give yourself 20 points for the right answer.
DOUBLE DARE: 1. The kickoff
2. Bill Cosby
Give yourself 40 points for the right answer.

9

We'd like to ask you a pointed question. So, point to any of these questions and answer it. Get the point?

DARE
1. In what war did the Yankees battle the Rebels?

2. On TV's *The Jetsons,* what is the name of George Jetson's son?

DOUBLE DARE
1. Cometophobia is the fear of what?
    A. Bicycle riding
    B. Comets
    C. Scrubbing sinks

2. In what city was the Declaration of Independence signed?

Are these quizzy questions driving you quazy? Then give the physical challenge on page 32 a try.

Then give the physical challenge on page 32 a try.

~~~~~~

Answers:
DARE: 1. The Civil War
2. Elroy
Give yourself 20 points for the right answer.
DOUBLE DARE: 1. Comets
2. Philadelphia
Give yourself 40 points for the right answer.

Knock, knock.
Who's there?
Anne.
Anne who?
Anne -ser a question right now!

DARE
1. What is the Roman numeral for 200?

2. Who is the author of *Blubber, Tiger Eyes,* and *Deenie?*

DOUBLE DARE
1. What chess piece can move in the most directions?

2. What is the name for the old-fashioned transportation device once known as the prairie schooner?

If you can't answer your question, it's time to move to page 33 for your brand-new, state-of-the-art physical challenge!

~~~~~~~~~~~~~~~~~~~~~~~~~~~~~~~~~~~~~

Answers:
DARE: 1. CC
2. Judy Blume
Give yourself 20 points for the right answer.
DOUBLE DARE: 1. Queen
2. Covered wagon.
Give yourself 40 points for the right answer.

11

It's the DOUBLE DARE name game. Name your question, then name names for the answer.

DARE
1. What is the name of the talking chair on *Pee-Wee's Playhouse*?

2. Name puppet star Punch's puppet partner.
- A. Sock
- B. Judy
- C. Harvey

DOUBLE DARE
1. The actress who plays Lauren, Alex's girlfriend, on *Family Ties*, got her start on Bruce Springsteen's *Dancing in the Dark* video. Name her.

2. Name the comedian who says he gets no respect.

If naming names isn't your thing, try the physical challenge on page 34.

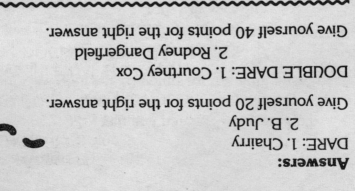

Give yourself 40 points for the right answer.
2. Rodney Dangerfield
DOUBLE DARE: 1. Courtney Cox
Give yourself 20 points for the right answer.
2. B. Judy
DARE: 1. Chairry
Answers:

Here's a DOUBLE DARE poetry break!

In DOUBLE DARE, one thing's for sure.
Answering the question is no bore.
Give the right answer and add some more
to your super DOUBLE DARE score.

DARE

1. If you are driving 60 miles per hour, how many miles per minute are you driving?

2. What do President Coolidge and the jeans designer named Klein have in common?

DOUBLE DARE

1. Let's try some musical multiplication. Multiply the number of strings on a cello by the number of strings on a violin. What do you get?

2. True or false: The musical *West Side Story* is set in Los Angeles, California.

If you can't answer your question, it's time to take the physical challenge on page 35.

~~~~~~~~~~~~~~~~~~~~~~~~~~~~~~~~

Answers:
DARE: 1. One
2. Their first names—they are both Calvins.
Give yourself 20 points for the right answer.
DOUBLE DARE: 1. $4 \times 4 = 16$
2. False. It takes place in New York City.
Give yourself 40 points for the right answer.

13

Pick any one of these. But be careful. These questions can mean trouble!

DARE
1. What kind of animal does a toreador fight?

2. Which is not a real place?
A. Santa Claus, Indiana
B. Grinch, New Mexico
C. Paris, Maine

DOUBLE DARE
1. What color are Superman's boots?

2. How many ears does an earthworm have?

Are these quizzers making you a little testy? Why not try the physical challenge on page 36?

14

These four questions are very tough. Try them out and show your stuff!

DARE

1. What are dachshunds, collies, and Chihuahuas?

2. What is the shorter distance—five kilometers or four miles?

DOUBLE DARE

1. Who draws Garfield?

2. What rock star is nicknamed "The Boss"?

Have you got a real pain in the brain? Stop brain drain—try the physical challenge on page 37.

∿∿∿∿∿∿∿∿∿∿∿∿∿∿∿∿∿∿∿∿

DOUBLE DARE Fast Fact: Harvey is really Harvey's last name! The full name of the announcer on DOUBLE DARE is John Harvey. Harvey is a well-known DJ in Philadelphia. He calls his radio show *Harvey in the Morning*.

∿∿∿∿∿∿∿∿∿∿∿∿∿∿∿∿∿∿∿∿

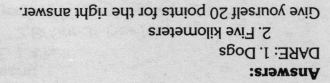

Give yourself 40 points for the right answer.

2. Bruce Springsteen

DOUBLE DARE: 1. Jim Davis

Give yourself 20 points for the right answer.

2. Five kilometers

DARE: 1. Dogs

Answers:

15

Check it out! Check it out! DOUBLE DARE questions going really cheap. Answer 'em while they last!

DARE
1. Rubies are red. Emeralds are green. Sapphires are usually what color?

2. What kind of animal is Baby Shamu?

DOUBLE DARE
1. Name the TV family ALF lives with.
2. Hieroglyphics are the written language of what ancient land?

If you don't know the answer, or you're looking for physical fun, try the physical challenge on page 38!

∧∧∧∧∧∧∧∧∧∧∧∧∧∧∧∧∧∧∧∧∧∧∧∧

DOUBLE DARE Fast Fact: It may be a small world, but the hardest questions for kids to answer on DOUBLE DARE are geography questions.

∧∧∧∧∧∧∧∧∧∧∧∧∧∧∧∧∧∧∧∧∧∧∧∧

Answers:
DARE: 1. Blue
2. Whale
Give yourself 20 points for the right answer.
DOUBLE DARE: 1. The Tanners
2. Egypt
Give yourself 40 points for the right answer.

Pick any one of these questions and give it a shot.

DARE

1. Which is not a fruit?
A. Avocado
B. Fig
C. Rhubarb

2. What were the three building materials the Three Little Pigs used to build their houses?

DOUBLE DARE

1. In your body the cerebellum is part of which organ?

2. A centennial anniversary is celebrated after how many years?

Did your question start bogglin' your noggin? Then try the physical challenge on page 39 instead.

~~~~~~

Answers:
DARE: 1. Rhubarb
2. Straw, sticks, and bricks
Give yourself 20 points for the right answer.
DOUBLE DARE: 1. The brain.
2. 100
Give yourself 40 points for the right answer.

17

It's the deal of a lifetime! Choose any one of these exclusive questions, and it's yours—to try and answer, of course!

DARE

1. What are Arabians, Morgans, and palominos?

2. Sour, bitter, and sweet are three of the four taste areas on your tongue. What is the fourth?

DOUBLE DARE

1. TV math time! If you multiplied the number of castaways on *Gilligan's Island* by the number of *Brady Bunch* kids, how many TV characters would you have?

2. In Greek mythology, what was Hydra?
   A. A many-headed monster
   B. A one-eyed giant
   C. A cream-filled cookie

If your level head has been leveled by these DOUBLE DARE questions, never fear. You have a chance to make up the points with the physical challenge on page 40.

~~~~~~~~~~~~~~~~~~~~~~~~~~~~~~~~~~~~~~~

Give yourself 40 points for the right answer.
2. A. A many-headed monster
DOUBLE DARE: 1. 7 × 6 = 42
Give yourself 20 points for the right answer.
2. Salty
DARE: 1. Horses
Answers:

18

These DOUBLE DARE questions were designed with you in mind.

DARE

1. "As Long as We Have Each Other" is the theme song from what TV show?

2. What is the official language of Germany?

DOUBLE DARE

1. What is the official language of Israel?

2. True or false: William Shakespeare was born in France.

If you're feeling really sporty, and want some fun, try the physical challenge on page 41.

try the physical challenge on page 41.

Answers:
DARE: 1. *Growing Pains*
2. German
Give yourself 20 points for the right answer.

DOUBLE DARE: 1. Hebrew
2. False. He was born in England.
Give yourself 40 points for the right answer.

Here's a major mix of DOUBLE DARE questions.

DARE
1. What is the capital of the United States?

2. Name the fourth Beatle: Ringo Starr, Paul McCartney, John Lennon ...

DOUBLE DARE
1. If you ordered dessert à la mode, what would be on top?

2. On *Pee-Wee's Playhouse,* what character gives Pee-Wee the secret word each week?

Feeling brave? Why not try to earn your points by taking the physical challenge on page 42.

~~~~~~~~~~~~~~~~~~~~~~~~~~~~~~~~~~~

DOUBLE DARE Fast Fact: The DOUBLE DARE writers have come up with 6,000 questions for the show!

~~~~~~~~~~~~~~~~~~~~~~~~~~~~~~~~~~~

Answers:
DARE: 1. Washington, D.C.
2. George Harrison
Give yourself 20 points for the right answer.
DOUBLE DARE: 1. Ice cream
2. Conchy
Give yourself 40 points for the right answer.

taking the physical challenge on page 42.

These questions are really deep! But you can dive right into them. Go ahead, take the plunge!

DARE

1. How many states in the U.S. have names that begin with the letter F?

2. In Madame Tussaud's famous London museum, what are all the figures made of?

DOUBLE DARE

1. In baseball, what is a full count?

2. Hey, hey! What is the last name of Davy, one of the Monkees on TV?

Can't answer the question? Don't know what it might be? Get to the physical challenge on page 43.

~~~~~~

Answers:
DARE: 1. One, Florida
2. Wax
Give yourself 20 points for the right answer.
DOUBLE DARE: 1. Three balls and two strikes
2. Jones
Give yourself 40 points for the right answer.

Questions, questions, questions ... Have you got the answers, answers, answers?

DARE
1. From the mean movie monster category, what kind of shark was the bad guy in *Jaws*?

2. What animal is a grown-up gosling?

DOUBLE DARE
1. What table spice comes from the berries of the *Piper nigrum* plant?
    A. Pepper
    B. Salt
    C. Sugar

2. What movie bad guy did Dr. Jekyll turn into?

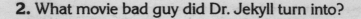

Are you stumped? Then turn to page 44 for your personalized DOUBLE DARE physical challenge.

Then turn to page 44 for your personalized DOUBLE DARE physical challenge.

Give yourself 40 points for the right answer.
2. Mr. Hyde
DOUBLE DARE: 1. A. Pepper

Give yourself 20 points for the right answer.
2. Goose
DARE: 1. Great white
Answers:

DOUBLE DARE's got the questions. You've got the answers. What a pair!

DARE
1. Name the primary colors.

2. What do you call the white of an egg?
   A. Yolk
   B. White glop
   C. Albumen

DOUBLE DARE
1. What does it mean if you wave a white flag in battle?

2. What ocean is directly off Canada's east coast?

If your brain is strained, try the physical challenge on page 45.

Give yourself 40 points for the right answer.
2. Atlantic Ocean
DOUBLE DARE: 1. I surrender. I give up.
Give yourself 20 points for the right answer.
2. C. Albumen
DARE: 1. Red, yellow, blue
Answers:

**On DOUBLE DARE the physical challenges
can get pretty physical!**

Chapter Two

LET'S GET PHYSICAL

Question: What makes DOUBLE DARE double the fun of any other show?

Answer: That crazy DOUBLE DARING display of physical fortitude, the physical challenge.

This chapter is filled with physical challenges just like the ones on DOUBLE DARE. You don't need a lot of supplies to try the challenges, all you need is a lot of nerve! Many of the challenges are designed to be done with a partner. But there are special instructions on each page if you want to take the challenge alone.

If you're playing DOUBLE DARE and keeping score, give yourself 40 points for each challenge you do successfully. Then follow the instructions on the bottom of the page. They'll get you back on the right track for your next DOUBLE DARE question.

Airmail

We'd like you to mail a few letters for us—airmail!

You will need:
    5 paper airplanes that you make yourself
    1 shoebox

Time limit: 20 seconds

The play: For this challenge the shoebox will be our DOUBLE DARE mailbox. Stand your mailbox on its side and place it on a table or a chair. All you have to do is get one airplane into the mailbox before the time is up. Remember, this is a short flight. You have only 20 seconds! If you're playing with a partner, you can both fly the planes.

Challenge for one: If you are playing alone, give yourself five more seconds.

If you did the challenge successfully, give yourself 40 points. Then try a question on page 6.

DOUBLE DARE Fast Fact: How do they think up the physical challenges on DOUBLE DARE? They actually think of a title first! Then they think of a stunt to go with it!

Paper Chase

Here's hoping you're full of hot air for this one.

You will need:
1 sheet of toilet paper

Time limit: 15 seconds

The play: You and a partner must work together to keep a piece of toilet paper in the air for 15 seconds. You can use only your breath to keep it flying. If the paper falls, you have to start all over again. You get three tries.

Challenge for one: If you're trying this on your own, give yourself an extra try.

If you didn't "blow" it, give yourself 40 points and try one of the questions on page 7.

DOUBLE DARE Fast Fact: Did you know that the writers and producers of DOUBLE DARE test out all the physical challenges themselves? According to producer Geoffrey Darby, "We get messier than anyone on the show, because often it doesn't work before it works!"

Egg-zact Timing!

You'll have to be an egg-spert to do this egg-citing physical challenge!

You will need:
    6 Ping-Pong balls
    1 empty egg carton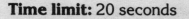

Time limit: 20 seconds

The play: Place the egg carton on a table or chair, four feet away from the throwing line. All you and your partner have to do is toss the balls into the carton. Get three in, and you win! If not, the yolk's on you! You have only 20 seconds to complete this task. Don't crack under the pressure!

Challenge for one: If you're trying this on your own, give yourself an egg-stra bonus of five seconds.

We'll stop shelling out these bad egg yolks so you can add 40 points to your score and then try a question from page 8.

Teamwork is the real key to success on
DOUBLE DARE.

Loony Balloony!

You'll get a bang out of this challenge!

You will need:
   4 balloons
   4 12-inch pieces of string

Time limit: 15 seconds

The play: Tie each balloon to a string. Then tie two balloons to one of your ankles and two to your partner's ankle. All you have to do is pop each other's balloons before the time is up. But be careful, this isn't a hands-on kind of physical challenge. You can only use your feet.

Challenge for one: If you are trying this alone, tie two balloons to one foot. Use your other foot to pop the balloons. It's not as easy as it sounds.

If you popped them all, give yourself 40 points, then pop over to page 9 for another slam-bang question.

DOUBLE DARE Fast Fact: More than 12 dozen balloons are used each week on DOUBLE DARE! (And did you know 12 dozen is called a "gross"? No joke.)

Back to Drool

Only on DOUBLE DARE is it okay to slurp your drink!

You will need:
　　2 plastic bowls filled with water
　　a small plastic or paper cup with a line drawn
　　an inch and a half from the bottom
　　2 straws

Time limit: 30 seconds

The play: You and your partner each have a bowl of water and a straw. You have to fill the cup with water by slurping the water from your bowls with your straws and then squirting it back into the glass. You have 30 seconds to fill the glass past the line.

Challenge for one: Give yourself an extra 10 seconds.

If you've slurped it over the line, add 40 points to your score, then turn to page 10 for your next question.

If you've slurped it over the line, add 40 points to your score, then turn to page 10 for your next question.

Back to Back Basketball

DOUBLE DARE etiquette lesson: Never turn your back on your partner—unless you're backed into trying this physical challenge.

You will need:
   a rubber ball
   1 basket or shoebox set up across the room from start

Time limit: 30 seconds

The play: You and a partner have to carry the ball downcourt and dunk it into the basket. But it's a little tougher because you have to carry it between your backs! If you drop the ball, you have to start all over again.

Challenge for one: This one can't be done alone, so try the next challenge.

Did you score? Give yourself 40 points, then turn back to page 11 for a new question!

Appley Ever After

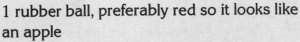

An apple a day may not always keep the doctor away, but it could earn you some big points. Here's how:

You will need:
> 1 rubber ball, preferably red so it looks like an apple
> a finish line (a belt lying on the floor)

Time limit: 20 seconds

The play: All you have to do is push the "apple" across the finish line. There are a couple of catches, though. You have to push the ball with your nose—because your partner will be holding your legs and wheeling you like a wheelbarrow, and you'll need your hands to help you "walk." Place the ball on one side of the room and the finish line on the other.

Challenge for one: If you are trying this on your own, slither over to the ball on your belly like a snake, push it with your nose and slither over to the finish line.

After this wheel-y tough challenge, a question from page 12 should seem as easy as apple pie!

Tie Breaker

This challenge will tie you up in knots.

You will need:
    1 sneaker with laces
    a blindfold

Time limit: 25 seconds

The play: Put on a sneaker and lace the laces. Easy, right? Well, not quite. You have to do it blindfolded. If you are playing with a partner, only one of you has to try the challenge.

All tied up? Give yourself 40 points and run over to page 13 for your next question.

DOUBLE DARE Fast Fact: All the kids who appear on DOUBLE DARE go through an audition with the producers. They have to answer questions and do a simple physical challenge. Sometimes they give the kids a different kind of test. They tell them one of the right answers they gave was wrong. They want to see how the kids will react. Will they just clam up? Will they get really angry? Or will they talk about it with their teammate? DOUBLE DARE wants kids who work together as a team.

Dress for Success

When it comes to fashion, DOUBLE DARE sets the trends! Here's your chance to dress for success!

You will need:
>1 oversized T-shirt
>1 adult-sized pair of jeans
>2 blindfolds

Time limit: 15 seconds

The play: One teammate wears the shirt, the other the pants. *You both wear your real clothes underneath.* And you both wear blindfolds. All you have to do is swap clothes before time is up.

Challenge for one: If you are trying this alone, wear the blindfold, take off your oversized clothes, turn them inside out, and put them on again.

If you aced this (after a fashion), give yourself 40 points. Then turn to page 14 for another DOUBLE DARE question!

Attack of the Killer Marshmallows

This game of catch is a real sweet treat!

You will need:
  10 marshmallows
  2 paper or Styrofoam cups
  2 blindfolds

Time limit: 20 seconds

The play: In this challenge you and your partner throw marshmallows at each other. You each have five marshmallows. You both hold a paper cup in your teeth. And, of course, you both wear blindfolds. Stand three feet apart. Ready, aim, fire! You each have to catch one marshmallow in your cup.

Challenge for one: If you are trying this alone, tape a cup, with the opening facing you, to a table. Wearing the blindfold, throw the marshmallows at the cup.

If you catch two, give yourself 40 points. Then turn to page 15 for a sure-fire question.

Baby's First Steps

You have to crawl before you can earn these points.

You will need:
1 Ping-Pong ball

Time limit: 20 seconds

The play: Get down on all fours balancing a Ping-Pong ball on your back. Crawl over to your partner, who is six feet away. Then put the ball on your partner's back. Your partner has to crawl back to the start. If the ball falls off, go back to start and try again.

Challenge for one: If you are trying this yourself, you must make both trips on your own, so give yourself five more seconds.

Did you do it? Add 40 points to your score, then crawl over to page 16 for a new question.

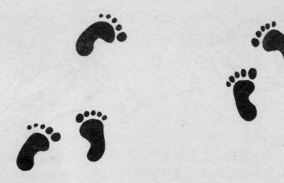

Hat Trick

Hats off to you if you pull this one off!

You will need:
    2 hats or caps, any type

Time limit: 20 seconds

The play: Sit on the floor facing your partner. You both wear hats. All you have to do is switch hats before the time is up. Here's the kicker—you have to use your feet to do the switching. (It helps to take off your socks and shoes.)

Challenge for one: You'd have to bend yourself in half to do this one, so try the challenge on the next page instead.

Did you make the big switch? Give yourself 40 points and tiptoe over to page 17 for your next question.

Orange You Glad You Came?

This physical challenge is fun and packed with vitamin C.

You will need:
   1 orange
   1 bucket or wastepaper basket

Time limit: 20 seconds

The play: All you have to do is take an orange and pass it to your partner, who dunks it in the bucket. But there is a catch. You have to keep your hands behind your back and hold the orange under your chin. Place the bucket five feet from where you start.

Challenge for one: If you're trying this on your own, the rules are a little different. Put the orange on a bed or couch. Kneel down and pick the orange up using only your head and chin. Carry it across the room and dunk it in the bucket.

Orange you glad that's over? Do you deserve the points or the pits? Give yourself 40 big ones. If you're hungry, eat the orange and turn to page 18 for more DOUBLE DARE fun!

Whistle While You Work

You know what you get when you put a bunch of ducks in a carton? A box of quackers, that's what!

You will need:
  5 crackers

Time limit: None

The play: Put all five crackers in your mouth. Then whistle "Mary Had a Little Lamb." Your partner just has to duck.

If you make it through the tune, give yourself 40 points. Then tune into page 19 for your next question.

DOUBLE DARE Fast Fact: The top money won by a team on DOUBLE DARE for answering questions is $750.

Checker It Out!

Everybody knows how to play checkers—but on DOUBLE DARE, we do things a little differently.

You will need:
    a checkerboard
    6 red checkers
    6 black checkers

Time limit: 15 seconds

The play: To earn the points, all you have to do is toss your checkers so that at least one red checker lands on a red square, and one black checker lands on a black square. Start by standing one foot from the checkerboard. Divide the checkers so that you and your partner each have six checkers. If you miss with all your checkers and time hasn't run out, pick them up and try again.

Challenge for one: If you are trying this on your own, you only get six checkers, but you only have to land one.

Check, please! Turn to page 20 for your next question. And remember, if you landed them right, you racked up 40 points.

DOUBLE DARE Soccer

Line up for the kraziest kickoff ever!

You will need:
1 blown-up balloon

Time limit: 20 seconds

The play: Everyone loves soccer — right? Well, DOUBLE DARE soccer works just like regular soccer. You have to kick the ball across the goal line. One player stands at one end of the room and kicks the soccer ball to the other. The second partner has to dribble it back and kick it past the goal line. Here's the DOUBLE DARE difference— the ball is a balloon.

Challenge for one: If you are trying this alone, you are doing double duty. Give yourself five more seconds.

If you reached your goal, add 40 points to your score. Then turn to page 21 for the next question.

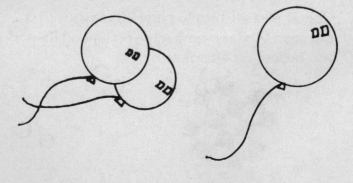

Two Heads Are Better than One

Get ready to put your heads together.

You will need:
    1 Ping-Pong ball
    1 plastic bowl

Time limit: 20 seconds

The play: Your job is to work with a partner to carry a Ping-Pong ball over to a bowl. There's nothing to it if you put your heads together. Just stand forehead to forehead with the ball in between, and walk over to the bowl. The bowl should be four or five feet away. Of course, if you drop the ball, it's back to the beginning again.

Challenge for one: Sorry, this is for twosomes only, but turn to the next page for a great solo challenge.

Did you make it? Give yourself 40 points. Now use your head to answer a question on page 22.

The Last Straw

You'll have a ball with this one.

You will need:
>   5 paper cups
>   2 Ping-Pong balls
>   1 straw

Time limit: 30 seconds

The play: You have to get the balls in the cups using lung power. Set the cups on their sides at the end of a table. The opening of the cups should be facing you. Use a straw to blow the balls across the table and into the cups. Ready! Set! Blow!

If you got both balls in the cups, add 40 points to your score, then go to page 23 for the last question of this round.

Blowing in the Wind

It's 40 points or bust in this challenge!

You will need:
   1 bottle of bubble stuff
   2 Ping-Pong paddles

Time limit: 20 seconds

The play: All you have to do is get a bubble over the finish line. Here's how you do it. Your partner blows a bubble, then both of you use your paddles like fans to try and make the bubble float over the line. The finish line should be six feet from where you start. Here's the bubble trouble: if your bubble bursts, you have to start all over!

Challenge for one: Blow your own bubbles, and give yourself some help. Make the finish line only three feet from the start.

If you got your bubble across, give yourself 40 points. Now total up all your points. This round of DOUBLE DARE is over, but you can start again with a new question on page 5. *Or* you can go on and try some of the super sloppy physical challenges in the next chapter.

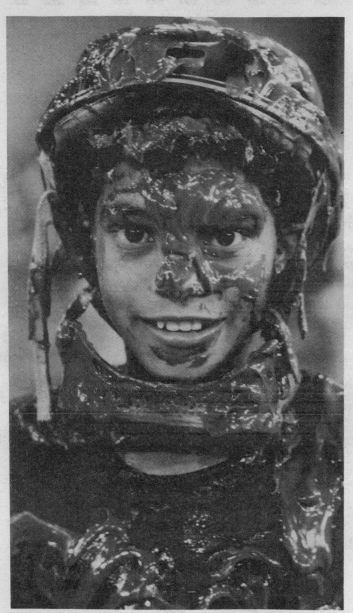

**On DOUBLE DARE everyone gets super
sloppy sometimes!**

Chapter Three

SUPER SLOPPY PHYSICAL CHALLENGES

When it comes to DOUBLE DARE, mess is best! But whatever you do, do these stunts outside and only with your parents' permission. Otherwise you could end up in a mess of trouble!

If you're keeping score, these physical challenges are all worth 40 points and can be done in place of any of the challenges in the last chapter. Or you can do them just for fun.

Splish Splash

Time to take a bath!

You will need:
a marking pen
2 paper cups
a chair (Make sure you have your parents'
permission. The chair is going to get wet.)
a bucket of water

Time limit: None

The play: First use the marking pen to make a
line about a third of the way up the side of one of
the cups. Now all you and your partner have to do
is pour enough water into the cup to come up to
that line. Here's how. You sit outside in a chair with
the bucket of water in front of you. Your partner
sits on the ground behind you with his or her back
to your back, holding the cup over either shoulder.
Now you use your cup to throw water over your
shoulder into your partner's cup. Have fun—and
don't forget to wash behind your ears!

If you filled the cup, add 40 points to your score
and get ready for more super sloppy fun!

Fill 'er Up

This physical challenge lets you pour it on!

You will need:
    a chair (Make sure you have your parents'
    permission. The chair is going to get wet.)
    1 paper cup
    1 plastic pitcher
    1 small hand mirror

Time limit: None

The play: Your partner sits on the chair—
outside, please—holding a paper cup on his
head. You stand with your back to him, holding a
pitcher full of water and a mirror. Use the mirror to
fix your aim, then pour the water into the cup. If
you wind up with at least one inch of water in the
glass, you win.

**DOUBLE DARE Fast Fact: DOUBLE
DARE uses 50 gallons of whipped
cream per day!**

It's a Scream!

This challenge will definitely get you in a lather, but give it your best shot.

You will need:
shaving cream in a push-button can
(Don't take Dad's without permission.)
a paper cup
sunglasses

Time limit: 20 seconds

The play: Here's the deal. All you have to do is fill a paper cup one quarter of the way full with shaving cream. You and your partner stand one foot apart. Your partner holds the paper cup with his or her teeth and wears the sunglasses to keep the gak out of the eyes. Now you shoot a stream of cream into the cup.

DOUBLE DARE Fast Fact: It only takes 20 minutes to clean up after each DOUBLE DARE taping.

Balloon-acy

Do this right, or you'll be all wet! And remember, do this outside only!

You will need:
> 15 water balloons
> a pair of oversized sweat pants

Time limit: 30 seconds

The play: You wear the pants in this one (over your real old clothes, of course). Your partner hands you the balloons, and you stuff them into your pants. Get them all in in time, and you can add 40 points to your score.

DOUBLE DARE Fast Fact: DOUBLE DARE is so super sloppy, it takes 15 people to clean up the set after each show is taped.

The food on DOUBLE DARE is *not* for eating!

Chapter Four

MESSY MUNCHIES AND SUPER SLOPPY FOOD

DOUBLE DARE fans are always ready to go for the goo! Especially when it comes to treats. If they're chocolatey, whipped creamy, messy-to-the-max, and daringly delicious, they're definitely for us! This chapter is loaded with fabulous DOUBLE DARE recipes that you can try. Just be sure you've got permission from the chief of the kitchen before you start. And always have an adult around if you're using sharp knives or turning on the oven. One more tip. Clean up when you're finished, or you could really be finished!

Enough about being neat — let's eat!

Funky Fondue

This fondue is a sweet treat for you. Here's all you do. (Bet you didn't know this was rhyme-time—whoops, there we go again. Will we stop? Who knows when!)

You will need:
>   chocolate syrup
>   banana slices
>   strawberries
>   apple slices

Here's what you do: Pour a big mess of chocolate syrup into a plastic bowl. Spear a piece of fruit with a fork, and dip it in the syrup. Keep dipping and eating until the fruit is all gone.

 DOUBLE DARE Fast Fact: There are 30 gallons of green slime on hand at every taping of DOUBLE DARE!

Rolling in Honey

This sticky sweet treat will drive you nuts!

You will need:

    1 cup of peanut butter
    1 cup of raisins
    ½ cup of honey
    1½ cups of shredded coconut
    1 teaspoon vanilla
    waxed paper

Here's what you do: Combine the peanut butter, raisins, and honey in a plastic bowl. Add the vanilla and mix well. Then spread the coconut on the waxed paper. Pick up handfuls of the honey-peanut-butter goop, and roll it into balls in your hands. Super sloppy can mean super sticky, too! Then roll the balls in the coconut. Put them on a plate or tray. Chill the candy for a few hours, and then they're ready to eat!

SUPER SLOPPY SUNDAES

These ooey-gooey sundaes are scrumptious on Sundays or any day! They are the grossest, sloppiest, mushiest, messiest, stickiest sundaes ever made—just right for you, the DOUBLE DARE kid!

Mud Slide Sundae

You will need:
chocolate ice cream
chocolate chips
whipped cream
chocolate sauce
chocolate sprinkles
1 cherry

Here's what you do: Start with two scoops of chocolate ice cream. Use a fork to mix in the chocolate chips. Cover the chips and ice cream with whipped cream, chocolate sauce, and chocolate sprinkles. Top the whole thing off with a cherry. This sticky, chippy, melt-in-your-mouth mud slide is a must for any DOUBLE DARE fan.

The Sundae Slide is one of the most difficult
obstacles on DOUBLE DARE.

Green Slime Split

You will need:
pistachio ice cream
chocolate syrup
whipped cream
1 banana
3 cherries

Here's what you do: Use a plastic knife to split the banana in half and put it in a long ice cream dish. Pile three scoops of ice cream on top of the banana. Add chocolate syrup, whipped cream, and cherries.

Aw, Nuts!

You will need:
vanilla ice cream
smooth peanut butter
chocolate sauce
whipped cream
unsalted peanuts
1 cherry

Here's what you do: Put two scoops of ice cream into a bowl. Use a fork to mix one tablespoon of peanut butter into the ice cream. Cover the peanut butter ice cream mix with chocolate sauce. Smother the whole thing in whipped cream and top with a few peanuts and a cherry. It's a little nutty, but a lot delicious.

Marshmallow Mess Ice Cream Soda

You will need:

    cherry soda
    chocolate ice cream
    mini-marshmallows
    whipped cream
    1 cherry

Here's what you do: Fill a glass halfway with cherry soda. Add one and a half scoops of chocolate ice cream. Pour in a few mini-marshmallows (remember, they get caught on your straw, so don't put in too many), and top with oodles of whipped cream. Finish the whole thing off with a cherry. A straw and a spoon are the perfect combo for this super slurpy delight!

A Piece of Cake

You will need:
    a piece of cake (any kind you like)
    chocolate chips
    banana slices
    vanilla ice cream

Here's what you do: Using a spoon, mix and mash all the ingredients together in a bowl until you've made one dripping, mushy, mashed-up mess. Then dig in! It looks gross, but this slop by any other name will taste as sweet!

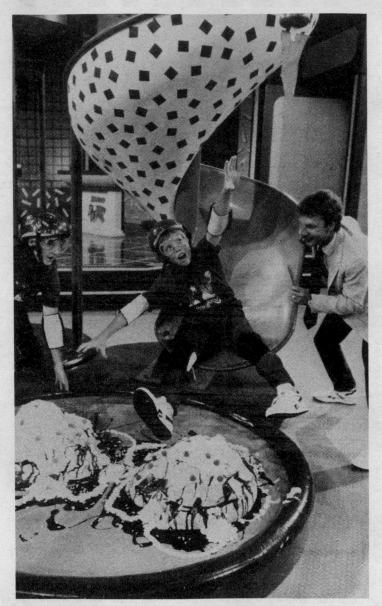

**A DOUBLE DARE contestant goes for it in
The Obstacle Course!**

Chapter Five

HAVE A DOUBLE DARE PARTY!

Every day's a party day on DOUBLE DARE!
Now *you* can have a DOUBLE DARE party in
your own home.

A DOUBLE DARE Welcome
▢▢▢▢▢▢▢▢▢▢▢▢▢▢▢▢▢▢▢▢▢▢▢▢▢▢▢

About a week before your party, get your pals in
the mood for a real blowout with these high-flying
invitations.

All you need is notebook paper, a pen, an indelible
marker, and balloons. On a sheet of paper write "I
Double Dare you to come to my DOUBLE DARE
party." Then write a note with your name, address,
and telephone number, as well as the time and
date of the party on it. Tell your friends to wear old
clothes.

Tear up more paper into pieces of confetti. Stick the note and the confetti into the balloon and blow it up. Once the balloon is tied, use the indelible marker to write "Pop Me!" on the balloon. Hand deliver these balloons to your guests. They'll be sure to get a bang out of them!

If you have to mail your invitations, here's another ballooning idea that's guaranteed to make your party a real blowout. Blow up a balloon. Hold it closed, but don't tie it. Use the indelible marker to write the time, date, and address of the party. Deflate the balloon and slip it into an envelope with a note that says "Blow Me Up!" When the balloon is blown up, the message will be clear.

Setting the Stage
❑❑❑❑❑❑❑❑❑❑❑❑❑❑

It's easy to turn your home into a D-lightful place for a DOUBLE DARE party. Start by making D-signs out of construction paper. Just cut out big D's from all different-colored pieces of construction paper, and tape them all over the room. Then hang bright balloons from the walls and the ceiling. Write the words DOUBLE DARE on a big piece of poster board, and hang it over the doorway. That's your DOUBLE DARE sign of approval.

When you're all through, we're sure your friends will grade your party room in all D's—for Definitely DOUBLE DARE Decorations, of course!

DOUBLE DARE Matchup

Get the DOUBLE DARE action going with this matchless match game. The game serves a double purpose. It gets the party going and gets your guests into DOUBLE DARE teams.

Before the party, get together a bunch of index cards and a bunch of colored markers or crayons. You'll need exactly half as many cards as the number of guests. (Stay tuned, you'll see why.) Write DOUBLE DARE on each card. Make the writing on each card a different color. Now, using blunt edged scissors, cut all the cards in half so that one half says DOUBLE and the other says DARE. Put the cards in a big bowl. When your guests come in, ask them to close their eyes and take a card. Once everyone has arrived at your party, tell your guests to walk around and find the person who has the card that matches theirs. In other words, a person with a red DOUBLE must find the person with the red DARE. The person with the blue DARE must find the person holding the blue DOUBLE. Each match is a DOUBLE DARE team.

Gag the Giggles Game

🔲🔲🔲🔲🔲🔲🔲🔲🔲🔲🔲🔲🔲🔲🔲🔲🔲

We know you're going to play DOUBLE DARE at your party, but here's a fun game to get everyone warmed up first.

This game is sure to have you rolling on the floor! Everyone sits in a circle on the floor. Pick one person to sit in the middle of the circle. The person in the center holds up a handkerchief. No, that person doesn't blow, that person throws—the handkerchief, that is! As soon as the handkerchief leaves the hand of the person in the middle of the circle, everyone else has to start laughing. The gang has to keep it up until the handkerchief hits the ground. Then all laughing must stop. Not even a snicker or a grin is allowed. Anyone who can't gag that giggle is *out* of the game. Keep going until just one person is left. He/she is the winner!

∿∿∿∿∿∿∿∿∿∿∿∿∿∿∿∿∿∿∿∿∿∿∿∿

DOUBLE DARE Fast Fact: The most disgusting thing ever on DOUBLE DARE was when they filled the tank with baked beans. Yuck! It took 150 cubic feet of beans. And it took a septic tank cleaner to get rid of the stuff!

∿∿∿∿∿∿∿∿∿∿∿∿∿∿∿∿∿∿∿∿∿∿∿∿

Fine Foods

ꟹꟹꟹꟹꟹꟹꟹꟹꟹ

If you're going to try all those tough physical challenges, you'll need some nourishment. Here are some ideas for quick snacks.

The Everything-but-the-Kitchen-Sink Super Sandwich

ꟹꟹꟹꟹꟹꟹꟹꟹꟹꟹꟹꟹꟹꟹꟹꟹꟹꟹꟹꟹꟹꟹꟹꟹꟹ

We DOUBLE DARE you to concoct the craziest, sloppiest hero sandwich the world has ever seen.

Place a pile of hero rolls on a table. Then lay out a spread of cold cuts, cheeses, lettuce, tomatoes, onions, mayo and mustard, and oil. It's up to your guests to create the great American hero! Remember, everything is allowed, except no silverware, please!

The Grossest, Gakkiest Desserts on Earth

ꟹꟹꟹꟹꟹꟹꟹꟹꟹꟹꟹꟹꟹꟹ

You know where to find these. Just turn back to the Super Sloppy stuff in Chapter Four!

The Obstacles, Of Course!

▱▱▱▱▱▱▱▱▱▱▱▱▱▱▱▱▱▱▱▱▱▱▱▱▱

There's no better way to end your party than the way DOUBLE DARE ends every show—with a race through a genuine DOUBLE DARE obstacle course. And because *THE DOUBLE DARE GAME BOOK* is doubly fun, you have two obstacle courses to choose from. The first one is fun but not-so-sloppy. The second is super sloppy and must be done outside, with the permission and help of a parent. The challenge—a team of two must make it through.

NOTE: On DOUBLE DARE you must make it through the obstacle course in 60 seconds— but in this version, just making it through will be enough of a challenge! The time limit is optional.

Here are some helpful hints on setting up your very own DOUBLE DARE obstacle courses.

1. Make sure you have plenty of room. The obstacles don't have to be very far apart, but remember, there are eight of them.

2. Be sure to set up the Super Sloppy Obstacle Course outside. Some of these things are really gakky!

3. Be sure to have all your obstacles set up beforehand. That way you won't have to stop the party to do it. One thing, though, be sure to leave the ice cream obstacles in the freezer until right before you start—melted ice cream is too sloppy—even for a DOUBLE DARE obstacle course!

4. Line up in teams of two. One team at a time will go through the course. Remember, just like on DOUBLE DARE, the two team members take turns doing the obstacles. Be sure to read the instructions to the right player for each obstacle.

5. Wear old clothes!

DOUBLE DARE Fast Fact: There are definitely tricks to getting through the obstacle course. The hardest obstacles are the ones where you have to find the flag in a mess of gak. Here's the trick. Spread your fingers like a fork and slowly comb through the gak. Most kids push their hands in and wind up pushing the flag around in the mess.

THE NOT-SO-SLOPPY OBSTACLE COURSE

The course is designed to be done by a two-person team. You can be the host and read the instructions to each team. Here they are...

Obstacle One: Daring Feet

You will need:
   9 odd socks
   1 matched pair of socks
   a laundry basket

The play: All the socks are mixed up and thrown into a laundry basket. You must find the matching socks and roll them up in a ball. Hand or toss them to your partner. Your partner must then run directly to...

DOUBLE DARE Fast Fact: All the drippy, messy food that is used on **DOUBLE DARE** is what they call "stale-dated" food. It's food that would otherwise be thrown out. **DOUBLE DARE** uses stale-dated food because the producers don't want to waste good food.

Obstacle Two: That's a Wrap

You will need:
1 small gift box
contact paper
a bow
a pair of blunt edged scissors

The play: Here's an obstacle you have to stick to till the end! All you have to do is gift wrap the box in contact paper. Of course, you have to peel the backing off the contact paper so that it's good and sticky. Finish off the gift wrapping with a bow. Then tag your partner so he or she can head to...

Obstacle Three: Same Old Grind

You will need:
a plastic spoon
a plate
an open can of coffee (Ask your Mom or Dad for that can of stale coffee that's usually hidden in the back of the cabinet.)
a plastic knife

The play: The coffee grounds should be poured into a bowl. The spoon is on the plate. Your job is to bury the spoon in the coffee. The only problem is, you have to use the knife as your shovel. You can't touch the coffee or the bowl with your hands. As soon as the spoon is completely covered, tag your partner and both of you race over to...

Obstacle Four: All Dressed Up, Four More to Go!

You will need:
a hat
a coat
1 large pair of jeans (Ask an adult if you can borrow a pair.)
1 large shirt
1 pair of adult shoes

The play: Every once in a while, DOUBLE DARE tries to make a real fashion statement. This isn't it. To play you must put the DOUBLE DARE clothes on over your own. As soon as you are dressed from head to toe, you may tag your teammate, who should run over to . . .

Obstacle Five: Special Delivery

You will need:
paper
pencils
a blindfold

The play: This is as easy as ABC. All you have to do is write a letter to your partner. The letter must have at least three words in it. Sounds easy. Well, nothing is ever as easy as it sounds on DOUBLE DARE. To get the DOUBLE DARE stamp of approval, the writer has to wear a blindfold. As soon as your partner reads the letter, he or she can move "write" to . . .

Obstacle Six: Cream Scream

You will need:

a spoon
a Ping-Pong ball
a large bowl
shaving cream (Be sure to get your parents' permission before you borrow it.)

The play: Here's the challenge. You have to use the spoon to find a Ping-Pong ball that has been buried in a bowl of shaving cream. Then you have to carry it on the spoon to your partner who will be waiting at . . .

Obstacle Seven: Pot Luck

You will need:

2 pot tops
6 or more Ping-Pong balls

The play: All you have to do is use the pot tops like cymbals and catch one Ping-Pong ball inside them. Your partner will throw the balls, and you will catch them. Stand four feet apart. When you've caught one ball rush right over to . . .

Obstacle Eight: Sundae School

You will need:
  - a plastic bowl
  - vanilla ice cream
  - a spoon
  - chocolate sauce
  - peanuts
  - whipped cream
  - a table

The play: The first player stands, hands on hips, facing a table. The second partner kneels behind the first and slides his or her arms through the first partner's arms. Now you have to work together to make an ice cream sundae. Only the kneeling partner can pick things up, but it's up to the standing partner to fill the kneeling partner in on where the fillings are! Get through this obstacle course, and sweet victory is yours! And of course you get to eat the sundae!

DOUBLE DARE Fast Fact: Here's the big trick for making the Human Hamster Wheel go: never look at your feet. If you look at your feet, you automatically stop climbing, and you can actually start making the wheel go backward!

THE SUPER SLOPPY OBSTACLE COURSE

Obstacle One: Pop Star

You will need:
    6 water balloons (fill them as full as you can)

The play: You must pop the water balloons by sitting on them. So, have a seat! As soon as one balloon pops, it's up to your partner to put the next one on the ground so you can pop it. But don't get too comfortable. This is no rest stop. As soon as all the balloons are popped, your partner should go directly to . . .

Obstacle Two: Nuttin' Special

You will need:
    peanut butter
    jelly
    bread

The play: Nuttin' to it. All you have to do is make a peanut butter and jelly sandwich. There's only one catch. You can't use any silverware. Spread it around with your fingers. Cover with second piece of bread, then pass the sandwich to your partner, who should go directly to . . .

Obstacle Three: Make a Splash

You will need:
> a large plastic bowl filled with water

The play: Put the bowl on the ground. All you have to do is get all but the last inch of water out of the bowl. Splash it out. Use your hands as a cup, try anything. But you cannot tip or move the bowl. Once the bowl is empty, tag your partner, and he or she can head for . . .

Obstacle Four: I Want My Mummy!

You will need:
> 3 rolls of toilet paper (Be sure to get your parents' permission first.)

The play: You must stand absolutely still while your partner wraps you in toilet paper from head to toe. Do it as fast as you can, so the wrapper can run to the next obstacle. That will give you a few seconds to break loose and join your partner at . . .

Obstacle Five: The Big Squeeze

You will need:
a paper cup
4 oranges—cut into quarters (Better let an
adult do the cutting. You save your strength.)

The play: Stand about four feet from your partner.
One partner is the thrower, the other is the juicer.
The thrower tosses the orange slices to the juicer.
All the juicer has to do is catch the slices and
squeeze them into the cup. Fill the cup past the
one quarter full mark and go directly to ...

Obstacle Six: A Shave
and a Haircut ...

You will need:
a chair
goggles or sunglasses
shaving cream (Don't take without asking!)
a Popsicle stick
a towel

The play: Your partner sits in the chair wearing
goggles or glasses to protect the eyes. You cover
your partner's face with shaving cream. Then use
the Popsicle stick to "shave" your partner's face
clean. Once all the shaving cream is gone, the
shaved teammate should towel off and make a
clean break to ...

Obstacle Seven: Blind Side Blitz

You will need:
>   2 blindfolds
>   a large trash can
>   a football

The play: Get ready to score. One partner is the thrower, the other is the receiver; the thrower puts on a blindfold to throw the ball to the blindfolded receiver. The receiver tries to catch it in the can. The spectators will pick up missed balls and hand them back to the thrower. But it's up to you players to talk it up out there so that you know where to throw the ball. As soon as one pass is caught, rush right over to . . .

Obstacle Eight: Get the Scoop

You will need:
>   ice cream
>   an ice cream scooper
>   3 ice cream cones
>   whipped cream
>   3 cherries

The play: For this last obstacle, you both have to work together to make an ice cream factory assembly line. The first teammate puts the scoop into the cone. The second partner adds the whipped cream and the cherry to top off the cone. Don't worry about appearances. On DOUBLE DARE, neatness never counts! Finish this, and you've done it. Just get your last licks in, and you can eat the ice cream.